Poetry Reflections

Celebrating 80 wonderful years

(signature) March 27/23

Poetry Reflections

Celebrating 80 wonderful years

WARING JONES

Library of Congress Control Number: 2023900854

ISBN: 978-1-960093-10-3   (Paperback)
ISBN: 978-1-960093-11-0   (eBook)

Printed in the United States of America

Contents

Dedication

This February the 4th marks the four-year anniversary of my deceased wife, Kit. Through her love and belief in me, she saved me from myself. Before we reunited in 1989 (I had known her since she was three), I was a lost soul. Kit helped me to gain faith in myself by suggesting that I stop drinking. It was a game changer for me and for us. It can be summed up in a little verse I wrote.

> Letting go of the past
> And seeing what life has to give
> Allows us to continue forward
> So it doesn't slip by like a sieve

A Mother's Touch

A Mother's touch is always there
From the crib until the coffin
It always feels so loving
And you long to have it often

A Mother knows just what to say
No matter the occasion
Being suckled as a youngster
Or being fed a plump dark raisin

The loving voice inside her
Has a calm and soothing tone
Like a poet on his bended knee
As he reads his new love poem

A gentle arm around your shoulder
Stops the tears and gasping sighs
And your world goes back to normal
When you gaze into her eyes

Her loving eyes and warm embrace
Make scratches fade away
Remaining in your heart of hearts
Forever and a day

Hang onto all this loving
Never let it fade away
Keep it close for now and always
In your work and in your play

Let your Mother's touch be with you
When you hold her in your arms
And know the loving person you've become
Was from her loving charms

Acupuncture

Acupuncture calms my soul
It's such a hidden treasure
It's one of China's major gems
And gives me untold pleasure

I can't remember just off hand
It feels like it is legion
It's either two or three hundred
Or somewhere in that region

Whenever pain presents itself
In all its many ways
And lingers in my knees or arms
For many painful days

I take myself to find a cure
I know it will help what ails me
And acupuncture is that source
It never seems to fail me

My pulse is taken gently
One wrist and then the next
It's entered in my file
In a flowing Chinese text

I lay down on the table
With my clothes stacked on the chair
And feel the pain diminish
As she always takes such care

It really doesn't take that long
To find the source of pain
And when I leave her office
I'm once more as right as rain

Add (Dad)

I try to relate to things that I feel
The dreams, the thoughts, the things that are real
It doesn't turn out like it should all the time
But mostly, with patience, it all turns out fine

We all have our foibles. I know this is true
We all have our foibles between me and you
We all have our foibles; just look and you'll see
We all have our foibles between you and me

When questioned about my feelings and such
The answer I give is often "not much"
But how can that be the usual reply?
I shrug and I answer, "I don't know why"

I don't know why I keep butting in
When people are stating their views
I'm sure it must be frustrating for them
But I don't seem to pick up the cues

New thoughts are forming as words start to flow
They pop out of my mouth with no place to go
I try to hold back as best as I can
But they still keep on coming without any plan

There is no fix; there is no potion
My thoughts are short-term with surface emotion
They flit, they flee, they jump, they bobble
It makes me tired; it makes me wobble

How can I love myself and find some self-esteem?
When thoughts are scattered and oh so lean?
I will try to rein in whenever I can
But it sure is hard for an ADD man

Christmas 2004

Alone With My Thoughts

Whenever I'm alone
And I'm dealing with my heart
I always turn to you, dear friend
To get a brand new start

You are the start and finish
Of all my waking days
The bottom and the apex
That keeps me in a haze

The beginning and the ending
Of thoughts that dwell on you
The lace inside the eyelet
As I tighten up my shoe

The many thoughts I have each day
Are slanted in your favour
And when choosing what dessert to have
I often choose your flavor

When two are one and separate
It can sometimes get confusing
It is hard to tell the difference
From a thought or simple musing

I don't seem to have a problem
When you are on my mind
My thoughts often revert to you
And how you are so kind

You are as kind as kind can be
And your words a perfect blend
And I realize the chosen words
My lover, my partner, my friend

Amazon Listing

My book is listed on Amazon
It is very exciting indeed
I just hope that you enjoy the book
And it turns out to be a good read

With all the work and effort I gave
And the hours of time that I spent
To see the title in black and white
Seems to me to be "Heaven Sent"

I know that my spirits are way above norm
That seems to be par for the course
But seeing the book in its' finished form
Leaves me with no time for remorse

I hope that the public will read and enjoy
The words that I tried to convey
And not cast aside like an old worn out shoe
The tale that I tried to display

The message it gives is simple for sure
So the children retain what they read
About sickness and health and how they relate
And not about malice and greed

The Christmas Spirit is still very strong
And children embrace it with glee
It's especially strong on Christmas day morn
With the presents spread under the tree

I'll never forget the glee that I felt
When my publisher called me to say
Your book is now listed for people to buy
And I know that it sure made my day

Backyard Garden

I went to visit the garden this morn
And not for the beets or the tall stocks of corn
But to see how the chives and onions have grown
In hopes that the seeds were carefully sewn
It doesn't take much to see gardens flourish
Just water and hoe and feed lots to nourish
The plants do the rest and like magic appear
And not just once but year after year

Our garden of life is much the same way
We walk, and we talk day after day
In order to flourish and make our lives strong
We all need to know what's right and what's wrong

Sometimes thoughts occur that help us feel right
That strengthens and nourishes us all through the night
And when morning draws near and our eyes open wide
We soon realize that we're the new guide

We have found a new path that our thoughts can embrace
That helps us belong in this marvelous chase
A chase to find love and kindness galore
As we constantly clamour to even the score

The score always seems elusive at best
As if we are writing a long-learned test
A test to determine our place on this earth
So that we can feel happy and stuffed full of mirth

I know that my garden of life brings me joy
No need to feel daunted, disgruntled, or coy
Just full of the gifts I've been given to share
Makes me ever thankful to show how I care

Being with Kit at Oak Bay Lodge

Her eyes are open and staring
At what I will never know
She still hasn't glanced towards me
So that I can feel her glow

Her head has yet to turn
To the left or to the right
I've been hoping that she might see me
And put me in her sight

Her left-hand rests on her tummy
Her right-hand is clasped in mine
She sometimes squeezes it gently
Which always makes me feel fine

So many times, she drifts to sleep
And I feel that it is the end
But her chest keeps slowly rising
So, she still has time left to spend

Her mouth is open like a chick in a nest
As she waits for her last breath of air
I sponge her lips with water
And to me, it never seemed fair

I will sit here beside her "till death do us part"
Though her eyes are locked in a stare
It's the least I can do for a lady, so fine
And it shows her how much I still care

It's time to go home now and garner some rest
I'll be back in this chair come what morn
Her time is in limbo on this Friday eve
And I don't want to feel so forlorn

Contemplative thoughts about Kit and her demise

Bicycle Poem

When you first begin to peddle
You must try hard not to mettle
With the energy inside you
That is trying to get out

So relax and let it flow
You've got nowhere else to go
Just keep pumping as before
And you'll find you will succeed

As the energy keeps flowing
You're content and also knowing
That the muscles that keep pumping
Are refined and doing well

So you keep on with the action
Because your tires have great traction
And you've entered in this contest
To complete it to the end

When the final gate is entered
Both your heart and soul are centered
And the threshold you've accomplished
Is a goal to make you proud

You have ridden hard for Cancer
And you still don't know the answer
But at least you tried your hardest
And that's all that one can do

Black Lives Matter
June 6 2020

"Please I can't breathe" is a catch phrase today
Summed up in the words BLACK LIVES MATTER
It has taken over the airwaves
And is not just some idle chatter

Each life on this planet is special
We all have our own lives to live
And when death comes to take us forever
We all gave the best we could give

Each person is sacred regardless of colour
Our thoughts and emotions are one
We wake in the morning with thoughts on our lips
And delighted to see the hot sun

I was raised by a father as brown as a berry
And a mother as white as the snow
I never thought much of the difference
For the love I received was a glow

My aunt and uncles were all very black
My grandfather was black as could be
Sometimes they told us their stories
That all seemed so foreign to me

My lineage is from a slave in the south
And the Underground Railway the source
Unusual to think of the troubles they had
But was actually par for the course

BLACK LIVES MATTER in how we proceed
Try not to think of the skin
Reflect on the courage it takes to go on
And you'll all be rewarded within

My grandfather was the first black teacher in Toronto, Ontario in 1923

Blue skies in the morning

Blue skies in the morning
Will continue for the day
Is the forecast that I love to hear
Cause there's nothing more to say

You know that you'll be blessed with sun
No matter what the task
And so your heart is filled with glee
And what more could you ask

The blue sky is the backdrop
For the sun, with all its power
So there is no need for raincoats
When there is no chance of shower

With sunny skies to light your day
Your tan is a pure delight
There is no need to watch for lines
It all turns out so right

With windows down and music high
You rise to the occasion
And set off for the sandy beach
With no need for strong persuasion

You trip the light fandango
As smiles come to your lips
Your arms are set akimbo
As they rest upon your hips

You doff your hat to those around
And set off in quite a hurry
You know there is no reason
To complain or whine or worry

Borje Salming

Borje was a friend of mine
That I met when nearing thirty-four
Maybe a little bit older
But I didn't really keep score

We were meeting at my place to go and play golf
Our tee time we had was for three
We left for the course altogether
As happy as happy can be

When choosing a golf cart companion
And a hero is part of the mix
There is a lot of fancy posturing
When trying to put in your fix

Robin's twelve-year-old son should ride shotgun, he said
In a voice full of love and great feeling
It's the right thing to do at this moment
And seemed to be most appealing

He never forgot the thrill of that day
Playing golf with a great hockey player
On top of the world for a few happy hours
He became a real dragon slayer

Many icons appear in our short time on earth
Very few make us stop and give pause
This moment will last forever
Enduring with such a great cause

Small gifts that are given with love
Can change how we picture our life
Our values become so much stronger
And negativity is cut like a knife

Braces

When looking at the different faces
I seem to see a lot of braces
They're part of growing up it seems
Like running shoes or denim jeans

They're not a stigma when you smile
But show that you have lots of style
You know when you are done with your teens
Your straightened teeth will shine and gleam

Before the braces did appear
You sometimes had an awkward fear
And wondered if the lasting view
Was something that was right for you

With counseling and tender care
You soon decided it was fair
And took the loving, warm advice
To try and make your teeth look nice

It started with a smallish tightening
That very soon was more enlightening
And now that you have lots of steel
It gives you such a strong appeal

They sometimes hurt when being tightened
I hope it doesn't make you frightened
But that you soon will realize
Your teeth are such a wondrous prize

The headbands on and some elastic
It makes you even more fantastic
Not that you needed that with me
You always fill our hearts with glee

A Bright Sunny Day in April

What can be better than a bright sunny day
As it welcomes us into the morn
Filling each nook with comforting light
And making us glad we were born

Born for this moment to take in the sun
With its powers just bursting with pride
As if it were saying to all who could hear
"Buckle down for this marvelous ride"

Open your heart to all that are near
And let them all know that you care
About what they are doing to keep themselves sane
And that you are delighted to share

Sharing is special in how it can heal
And brings joy that breaks down our fears
It helps us to know there are those who still care
And it keeps away all the salt tears

To share happy moments brings joy to our heart
And a smile that lingers like clay
Enjoying fond memories can gladden our soul
And bring joy for the rest of the day

Let the sun fill your heart till its breaking
There is room in a corner for you
A room that is touched by your kindness
And fits like a worn-out old shoe

No need to tread lightly when facing the day
Your love will do all the rest
And with help from your friends and neighbors
You'll realize that you are the best

Bronchitis

I've never had Bronchitis
But I hear it really hurts
Your fever rises up and down
And sometimes comes in spurts

Shortness of breath is common
And slight fever with the chills
And there is some chest discomfort
And not always cured with pills

A lot of rest seems helpful
But the coughing is quite nagging
And sometimes in the second week
You even end up gagging

I'd love to help you out my friend
But you're so far away
And with this awful sickness
You don't have much to say

I'll have to do the talking for
The two of us at present
And maybe with the poetry
It might turn out quite pleasant

I had a lovely birthday
And was busy all the day
I had my lunch and dinner paid
So it all turned out okay

I hope that I can chat with you
When you are fit and able
And we'll share some drinks together
And play footsie at the table

WARING JONES

Cabin Fever

The loneliness keeps creeping in
As if it owns my soul
And tugs at every corner
Like a long-forgotten scroll

I've tried to fight against it
But it's still a losing battle
My friends have seen the difference
And I hope that they won't tattle

The time goes by so slowly
For many months on end
A good book helps to calm me
Not like a loving friend

My thoughts that once were hidden
Start to bubble to the brim
They keep changing as the days go by
Seeming sluggish lost and thin

A new horizon comes into view
Each time I step outside
I welcome every nuance
And am glad to take the ride

A ride that sets my spirit free
To wander on its own
And wait for new adventures
Like a verse inside a poem

I'm ready for the walls to crack
And let some light shine in
And welcome all the hugs I get
With one big Cheshire grin

Cabin Fever Number Two

Is cabin fever just a state of mind?
Or is it a world of its own?
A world that is filled with sadness
And where we cannot roam

Where happiness has lost its way
And the map is hard to find
The streets end up as cull de sacs
Inside our twisted mind

The loneliness seems endless
With friends nowhere in sight
And nighttime lasts forever
So you just give up the fight

A fight you never started
And you feel you just can't win
Encapsulates your feelings
Full of sadness and chagrin

The still small voice of reason
Pokes its head through clouds of gray
Enlightening the mood you've cast
To let you have your say

The feeling slowly starts to grow
Each time you start a smile
And blossoms like a cherry tree
To go the extra mile

A mile that will shape your life
And turn your thoughts around
And let you know that you have gone
From lost to being found

WARING JONES

Caring

Don't wait to tell your loved ones
The way you really feel
You will benefit forever
And remain on even keel

Who doesn't like a hug at dawn?
To help us through the day
It's just the same as talking
But expressed another way

A small tap on the shoulder
Sends a spark down to our toes
And soon ignites a passion
That accelerates and grows

The still small voice we yearn for
That invades our evening prayers
Brings us comfort and serenity
To show how much He cares

The mother's touch is real my friends
We all have felt the caring
Of two loving arms around us
Bringing meaning to her sharing

Let's pass it on to others
Who deserve our love so deep
To enrich them and enrich us
When we're dreaming in our sleep

Harmony and love abide
For us to spread around
There's no need to keep on searching
It is cheaper by the pound

Carol

The drops are in your days begun
So now it's time to have some fun
Reflecting on the days gone by
Before the drops were in your eye

Your life-- like most-- is not one season
With nothing wrong but fraught with reason
Which strengthens us as we progress
To coddle us when in duress

Thank heaven sorrows touch our soul
So we are strong and take control
When havoc rears its' ugly head
We're not left out and full of dread

The many problems you are facing
You face head-on with no debasing
The hurts that linger in the past
Now dissipate and hardly last
Your children know your inner strength
That you will go to any length
To assist them with your endless love
Your hand inside their velvet glove

Pen Pals do not reflect our time
When ice cream only cost a dime
When hot dogs actually tasted good
Filled with real meat as well, they should

Your daughter has a loving friend
You don't just sew; you also mend
Your garden will be full and bright
You're doing everything that's right

Grieving a sick child

When your child is very sick
And confined to stay in bed
It fills you up with horror
And unbridled parent dread

Your senses and your actions
Seem to grind into a halt
But very soon, you realize
It's really not your fault

You raised them with love
And a sense of what's right
And hope that your teachings
Will show them the light

It doesn't seem fair
In the grand scheme of life
That your child is chosen
For conflict and strife

A bitterness forms
That was not there before
And it makes you quite anxious
To even the score

But love soon prevails
And sets the keel straight
And helps you to see
That you just have to wait

The kindness of friends
Surrounds you with joy
And strengthens the love
That you have for your boy

Children in Love

Children don't ask to give you their love
They give it all out as a gift
And every time I receive that warm love
It always gives me a lift

It boosts my morale to the limit
My heart feels full to the top
I accept it from them completely
With no inkling to ever say stop

It never crosses my mind
To restrict this love that is free
It is wholesome as the new driven snow
And it all feels so right to me

A smile appears as they hand you a gift
A card or a letter that's written
It always seems drawn to perfection
From soft hands like a new baby kitten

I have kept many cards from my childhood
That I wrote or were written for me
They represent all different ages
From nine to a low age of three

An art piece tucked into a corner
Being saved so that others might see
Turns up unannounced in the back of your drawer
And your heart almost bursts with the glee

Your mind once again returns to that time
When the drawing was meant just for you
You sway with unbridled enjoyment
For the love that was honest and true

Christmas 2017

It's Christmas again on a cold dark night
The dark streets outside are all filled with white
It snowed last night upon the ground
And settled there without a sound

It's been many years since it happened last
Tradition seems a thing of the past
Each new day brings a change in status
We take it as is with faith and gratis

The snow built up in tiny white hills
Fluffy and soft and full of thrills
The children romped and played their games
Laughing and falling and calling out names

None of them was sure just how to proceed
With so much snow and so much need
A need to enjoy the blanket of white
That thrilled them so and lit their light

A light that many had long forgotten
And too many sweets that made them feel rotten
And yet the chorus of voices rang clear
From far and wide for all to hear

"It's Christmas" they yelled, "and we are so glad"
Not one of us is naughty, and none of us is bad
Just good girls and boys with time left to spare
And wanting to show how much we all care

We care for the spirit that Christmas emits
We've tightened our scarves and pulled on our mitts
I want to say thank you to all of you here
And wish you the best and a Happy New Year

Coffee

Two whole pounds of coffee
Does not go very far
When you drink it in the kitchen
And you drink it in your car

When you drink it in the shower
It gets diluted till it's weak
And by the time you've finished
It is time to take a leak

It doesn't mean you must resort
To drinking at the table
Or watching favorite TV shows
On the internet or cable

It's so delicious when it is steaming hot
You sometimes burn yourself
And so you place it back again
Or put it on a shelf

It doesn't really take that long
Till once again your ready
To drink the dark brown liquid
Cause it's made your hands quite steady

The jolt it gives each early morn
Gives signals to the body
It's time to rise and shine once more
No need to drink a hot toddy

Sometimes I miss my morning drink
When rushing out the door
And take my turn at Starbucks
To even out the score

What a great elixir of life coffee has become for so many of us.

WARING JONES

Communicating

Phoning and texting are wondrous inventions
We use them and know they are real
They have been part of our lives for many years now
But don't always express how we feel

Phoning for me is my own special choice
I prefer it more often than others
It's my go-to way of saying I care
And I use it when I have my druthers

When you and I talked on the phone last night
My senses were revved and in tune
Certain phrases you said were delightful to me
And it felt like a hot day in June

Now I don't expect this to always be true
But alas, it sure would be grand
To know that each time our voices combined
It would be just like holding your hand

The cadence of language is special to me
The highs and the lows brought together
Help to keep me on track with what to say next
About music, or sports, or the weather

We are old in our age but still young at heart
About dating to find the "right one"
It is awkward and stressful and lovely of course
And is mostly just having great fun

I enjoy when you're near, and our hands almost touch
It reminds me of good times I've had
It helps me to see how lovely you are
And inside, I feel happy and glad

Covered in Covid

It's been quite a while since I've written a poem
Now that COVID directs what we do
I'm not really sure when my lace comes untied
If I can even tie up my own shoe

All the rules that exist to keep us all safe
From a virus we can't even see
Keeps us all on our toes of what will come next
So we have an idea what will be

Do I wear a new mask in my car all the time?
Or will the old one be fine when I'm driving
Should I wash my hands twice before I sit down?
So I still have a chance of surviving?

These questions abound wherever I go
And they seem to be part of our sole
No time to ponder what fate has in store
About crowds or just plain rock and roll

No groups are allowed to gather at will
And to form friendly bonds as before
We must all stay apart to keep ourselves safe
Or we might end up dead on the floor

I wonder how long this virus will stay
And keep the whole world in a tizzy
Always fearful to touch in case we get sick
Or stand up much too fast and get dizzy

This sickness will pass just like others before
And history will write the last line
And no matter what happens from now until then
We all will end up feeling fine

Thoughts about Kit in her new home forever more

She greets me with a great big smile
Which helps me go the extra mile
I know that she is safe at home
With long wide halls that she can roam

I hope her life is full of gladness
And that she sees no more of sadness
But simple joys that make her smile
And make her stay seem all worthwhile

I kept her home for far too long
Believing I was acting strong
It all became a great big mess
So I will try to not digress

Sometimes I visit once or twice
Sometimes I visit even thrice
It helps to keep away the sorrow
And lets me face a new tomorrow

We lived so many years together
Through sun, and sleet, and stormy weather
And even when we felt despair
We forged ahead and did repair

How could I know which thoughts to ponder
To stay on track and not to wander
To try and keep my spirits bright
To face the long and lonesome night

I thought the crying was all over
But it's really just begun
The sadness that was all around
Has finally seen the sun

I love you "My Little Jonsey
My Bag Of Bonsey "

Kit was admitted on February 20th at 10:30 A. M. 2015
To Oak Bay Lodge forever
It was the hardest task I have ever performed

My Doctor

My Doctor is a gentle soul
Who tries his best to keep me whole
To find the parts that hurt me most
Then fix them like a gracious host

He enters with a lovely smile
Which makes the waiting seem worthwhile
He listens to some woes and pains
And also for some hopeful gains

He straps the cuff around my arm
And does it with a graceful charm
He pumps the bulb until it's tight
Then checks again to see it's right

He's talking in a soothing fashion
Not using words with any ration
But coaxing out why I am here
So he will know which way to steer

I reel off what's on my mind
He listens trying to be kind
To assess what happens next
So he will have the proper text

He prods and pokes my body and mind
Just checking to see what he might find
Will there be issues easily attended
Or will my life become upended

The examining room is left behind
The windows have their shuttered blind
His counseling has assuaged my fears
And left me smiling and not in tears

Thank you Dr. Govender for being a great Doctor.
You continue to give me real and moral support

Don't Wait

Don't wait for the rainbow to brighten your day
You'll be waiting from dusk until dawn
The pot of gold is within you
To relish and draw fully upon

Good luck is just a figure of speech
That we use to make us feel good
In hopes that good fortune will follow
And help us to feel understood

Luck I am sure we make for ourselves
Each day as our feet hit the floor
We stand and take measure of what to do next
And set out for the day to explore

Should we go for a walk to loosen our limbs
Or a coffee to loosen our bowels
Both things are good for our psyche
And to help us find words for our vowels

Reach out to those who are near you
And to those you still haven't met
They are friends who are happily waiting
And will feel like they just won a bet

A bet that confirms all their feelings
Of friendship about to begin
The first step is already taken
That they know will end up a win-win

With each new acquaintance that enters your realm
A bond starts to form deep inside
You feel that a journey is starting to build
And you're glad that you jumped on the ride

The ride that you're taking is filled to the top
With love and kindness galore
And with each new horizon that enters your view
You stand up and shout "I want more"

Dreaming

You think that you are dreaming
But perhaps you're really scheming
To unravel all the mysteries
That are caged inside our minds

You reflect upon the choices
Cuz you think you're hearing voices
But it's only just the brain waves
That are bouncing uncontrolled

What's next you ask your inner self?
Should I be careful, do I need stealth?
Do I exceed my boundaries
Or should I continue on?

Of course there's no solution
Or a chance for absolution
When the images are changing
Like a Sunday matinee

You return to some illusion
That is mixed with mass confusion
And it's branded in your thoughts
That you have to carry on

Will dawn awaken and set me free
And know how things are meant to be
Or will the thoughts continue
To guide me on my way

I will have to hope my mind is steady
And my emotions fit and ready
For a new day soon is dawning
And my life will carry on.

WARING JONES

Early Morning Thoughts

The sky is gray—but not for long
The Robin has begun its song
She's resting now upon a tree
With eyes that focus just on me

I turn my head to watch her sing
Her colour is a wondrous thing
And as she sings with all her might
It fills my head with pure delight

Another bird alights quite near
It shows no outward sign of fear
It starts to chirp a steady song
With notes that are both short and long

The morning seems to come alive
With other birds that float and glide
They nestle near the lilac tree
Allowing me to watch and see

I take it in in one quick glance
A lovely form of happenstance
My very private warbling choir
That heats my heart like a roaring fire

This sound bite that has just occurred
Was never shaken never stirred
But happened in a captured time
Without a reason or a rhyme

Let's hope it isn't just today
Those birds come out to romp and play
But every morn when I arise
They'll start to sing and cloud my eyes

Easter Sunday

Many thoughts can cross our minds
When Easter is the topic
From dressing in your finest garb
To being philanthropic

Soup kitchens are a helpful way
To ease your troubled mind
To set the past behind you
And partake in something kind

It's easy in our busy lives
To keep on track each day
Not venturing outside our realm
And to try a different way

A different way to wear your hair
Or cook your meal at night
A different way to hug your spouse
To ensure that they're all right

A different way to help a friend
You've never helped before
Although they sometimes asked you
Cause they've always been so poor

A simple gesture never seen
Can guide you on your way
To open up a hidden door
And turn sad thoughts into gay

There is nothing wrong with chocolate
On this shinny Easter morn
But a hand extended gently
Makes you feel far less forlorn

WARING JONES

False teeth

Ten years ago I lost my teeth
But kept six around for good measure
They still had roots that stood the test
To guard an indentured treasure

It wasn't something new to me
To have my teeth removed
The dentist always told me
That my gums would be improved

When I was in my twenties
And my gums were oft infected
I'd open up my mouth quite wide
And they would be inspected

It's better that we cut your gums
So that your teeth remain
And over the next forty years
It was always the same refrain

One time the gums were cauterized
All quadrants cut together
And for the next two or three weeks
I stayed under the weather

Another time they cut them
And put stitches firm and tight
It proved to be quite painful
In the daytime and at night

I hope my few remaining teeth
Will hold up to the test
Allowing gums that seem quite fine
To finally get some rest

*I tried to sink my teeth into this subject but found that I just couldn't
Bite off as much as I wanted to chew.*

Feeling good

I have been feeling so good for so many years
I almost feel it's my right
To carry on working and spreading good cheer
Through the morning and into the night

I thought that my past might catch up to me
And throw me a curve ball or two
So my feelings of thinking I'm sacrosanct
Would be crushed like a soft warm cashew

Not that cashews are not good for eating
Believe me I think they taste great
And if graded by numbers from one up to ten
They'd come out at a very strong eight

I'm eating some now as I type out this poem
From a package I bought at half price
There are cashews and walnuts and filberts as well
And I might fry them for dinner with rice

What does any of this have to do with my feelings?
I am not really sure how I know
But as words come along and go down on this page
It sure helps my feelings to grow

I love all that I can from truth to ideas
And incorporate good feelings when able
I like to have them all lined in a row
The same as horses in an organized stable

Do you feel good about what you are doing?
I sure hope it's a positive vibe
And as morning progresses from noon until dusk
I welcome you into my tribe

Forever Together in Each Other's Arms

Forever together in each other's arms
Is the place that I long for the most
It feels so secure and so loving
Just like butter on freshly made toast

The warmth of our bodies rekindles the love
A love that is gentle and kind
And helps reaffirm the magic we share
As we both lay in rapture entwined

I never get tired of holding you close
So close that our hearts seem to touch
And in those few minutes of holding
I know why I love you so much

It's not just the sparkle your bright eyes emit
Or your smile so gentle and kind
It's your whole persona that makes me insane
As your lips drive me out of my mind

The time spent together these past sunny days
Makes my heart beat resound in my chest
And touching you gently each time that we kiss
Are the times that I enjoy best

We met as two strangers not seeking out love
But it found us and brought us together
And now that we share a love that is true
My mood is as light as a feather

I'm always excited each time that we meet
And I think of you morning and night
And for me my good friend I'm so thankful
That everything turned out so right

Forgiveness

It has taken me years to forgive myself
For some of the things I have done
Never realizing the hurt and the damage
That I simply perceived as just fun

Not caring that feelings were shattered
For a laugh or a moment of joy
Unaware of the hurt that I threw to the side
Like a bent and unwanted toy

Good friends take a long time to nurture
And need loving and caring to grow
But with patience and kindness as water
A beautiful flower will show

A flower so soft that it bends in the wind
But so hard that it stands straight and tall
A beacon of strength and of guidance
An example of love to us all

I cherish the friendship of those who are near
You guide me each night and each day
You help me to see the next step to take
And appreciate what I might say

My thoughts tend to ramble the older I get
And I hope it's a good sign of age
And as time slips through all of our fingers
Let us hope I wind up as a sage

Forgiving is hard if one can't let things go
And the healing won't start till you do
But once you decide that you're ready to start
The old person becomes a new you

August 23 2016

Can we ever quite imagine
What a loving cup has seen
And it's not just when it's dirty
But also when it's clean

So many lips have touched its' rim
Some soft and sweet like yours
But other lips are cracked and worn
And come from distant shores

The hands that wrap around the stem
Are sometimes coarse and rough
While other hands are delicate
And yet strong and very tough

The HARMONY of hand to cup
Is sometimes fraught with pain
While HUGS of GRATITUDE persist
To bring one home again

The cup of course holds many drinks
The likes we've never seen
And yet the liquid stays inside
And never will be seen

Is life much different than our cup
Which holds all that it's given
Until we try to break the bonds
And feel that we are striven

I know that you have filled me up
With love that I can't measure
You've helped me find my way again
And become my cherished treasure

August 24

I guess I just can't help myself
When writing silly lines
The words just keep on tumbling out
Surprising me sometimes

They float around inside my head
And end up on the page
Should I be locked up in a zoo
Or in a room like a cage

Time will tell if they make sense
Or if they have a meaning
I'll have to set some time aside
And do some careful gleaning

It doesn't seem to matter
What I put down on the paper
I have to clear my brain at once
So "better now than later"

Some wondrous thoughts are forming now
About a friend I know
And thinking of her in my arms
Makes all my senses glow

My body temp begins to rise
I'm taking off my sweater
It leaves me unrestricted
And I feel a whole lot better

Dearest friend you know by now
My thoughts are all on you
And we are bound together
With a magic loving glue

Friday Poem

My fingers are poised and ready to type
They're strong and the muscles are tense
My brain is revved up and dropped into gear
But as yet it doesn't make sense

Imagination is one of our last sanctuaries
That's what I've been told
So I'm trying my best to imagine
Lower case or dark and bold

Will there be theme this time around
Or should I make it random
Will it be in one long line
Or should it be in tandem

My thoughts are slowly turning
But they don't make any sense
They usually leap out of my head
Without fear of recompense

Perhaps it's time to spark some tinder
And wait for red hot fire
It might become a roaring blaze
Or a well stoked funeral pyre

The coals are burning slowly
I'm not sure what I should write
Will it be a new best seller
Or uninteresting and trite

I guess I just can't write today
My genius stays hidden
I'll try again tomorrow
And hope I will be bidden

We leave something of ourselves behind when we leave a place
We say that---even though we go away
And there are things in us that we can find again only by going there
We travel to ourselves when we go to places that we have covered a stretch of our lives
No matter how brief it may have been

Friendship

True friendship is lasting
And rare as hen's teeth
It comes with no strings
And is not a bequeath

A partially raised eyebrow
A smile oh so slight
Releases old memories
And sets the day right

I have such a friend
And he answers to Rick
Our feelings are mutual
With no deception or trick

Respect for each other
In work and in play
Makes our time spent together
To always seem gay

No yelling or sulking
Impedes our direction
And helps in the end
To succeed with perfection

This warmth that we carry
Has made both of us strong
With neither one caring
Who's right or who's wrong

I know it will last
Till the end of our day
And that my good friends
Is all I have to say

Frontotemporal Dementia

My wife it seems has FTD
That's not the way that life should be
She always tried to do her best
To fit in with the litmus test

But fate it seems has blocked her path
And filled her with a darkened rathe
That seems to let the brain keep shrinking
And not to let the thoughts keep linking

She's like a boat without a keel
A bicycle that has no wheel
And though there's lots of good intention
She doesn't have a lot to mention

She speaks in many numbers now
I'm not quite sure I don't know how
But they relate her thoughts to me
Of how she feels her life to be

She seems content throughout the day
And doesn't have a lot to say
But with her smile warm and bright
It takes the darkness from the night

As memory wanes and thoughts decline
You lose all sense of space and time
And enter into distant past
And hope those memories will last

I've done my best to keep her senses
Repairing only certain fences
And hope that I can try and find
Some way to keep her peace of mind

Written about my wife Kit Chilton 69

Golf

I always liked the game of golf
It really is a pleasure
You hit as far as you can hit
And then you start to measure

How many yards to hit the green
How many to the pole
How will I get around the tree
And will I sink the hole

So much of golf is how you swing
So much of it is guessing
So much is how you follow through
So much is just addressing

The part that I enjoy the most
Is being on the course
Just walking with a group of friends
And feeling no remorse

I like to play in early morn
When dew is sparkling bright
You set the ball upon the tee
And watch the ball take flight

You always hope for long and strong
Just for the rush that lingers
But often it falls very short
Misplacement of the fingers

You chip and putt around the hole
And miss it by a hair
But you are glad that you have come
You're with some friends who care

Green Hummingbird

Each early morning when I rise
And look through my kitchen glass
There's a hummingbird a buzzing
And it seems to have great class

It never hesitates too long
On one particular flower
It's not like I could leave the room
And take a long hot shower

I keep on watching from the sink
Out through the large glass pane
I think her name is Anna
And she's here for her refrain

I keep on reaching for my phone
To take her flight in action
But she is moving much too fast
I can't go no satisfaction

She darts around the corner
To suck on new found flowers
I guess I could be here all day
Or at least for five more hours

A feeding station might do the trick
To keep her in my view
I wonder if she'd use it
Or just count on morning dew

I'll try again tomorrow
When she flies into my sight
I know I'll catch a picture then
I'll try with all my might

Bird watching from my kitchen window
It thrills me to catch them in action

WARING JONES

Grey Morning Clouds

The stark moving clouds of the dark early morn
Look like mountains about to be formed
They are blocking the sun from doing its' job
Which is helping the earth to be warmed

A minute goes by or maybe it's ten
They have moved in a different direction
I was watching for change in what would appear
But alas I could find no detection

These massive grey swirls that form each new day
Remind me of nature's great power
They change in a second from strands to a cloud
And in minutes it's starting to shower

I never get tired of watching this game
That surfaces each early morn
It's like watching a canvas gets covered in paint
Or a child that is just being born

Creation-- in all of its wondrous forms
Makes me realize the chances we're given
To better ourselves at the start of each day
And enhance this great place that we live in

Hold hands with your partner and those you adore
It's not very long that we're here
So at least when you're gone your friends will all say
He gave us a great deal of cheer

Arise from the table and hug those you love
I'm sure that you'll get no rejection
Your friends will delight in your intimate ways
You have just done a deed of perfection

Grinning

What does it take to make you grin?
To keep you satisfied within
To make you go that extra mile
And finish with a winning smile

I try my best to grin and smile
It sometimes takes a little while
But after many times of trying
I never seem to end up crying

I guess I'm doing something right
I have my hearing and my sight
Although they're not completely mine
They still seem like they're doing fine

I guess with age we grin and bear it
And do our best to try and share it
And often when the day is done
We realize we've had great fun

We managed to collect some smirks
This keeps our laugh lines in the works
And helps to show our grace and style
And end up with a full-fledged smile

But grinning isn't just for me
That's not the way that fun should be
The fun that we desire often
Should make our neighbors' frown lines soften

Let's try to smile and laugh and dance
And sometimes maybe even prance
And if that action comes to pass
Kick up your heels and laugh and laugh

Halloween 2014 in Oak Bay

Thirty-six kids betwixt and between
Came up on my steps this dark Halloween
Some dressed like goblins and some dressed like kings
And some dressed like just about any old thing

Some knocks were like warnings of things yet to come
While others were happy and full of great fun
Some rang the doorbell and took one step back
Perhaps they were scared of a goblin attack

I donned my clown wig and put on my best smile
In hopes that perhaps they would linger awhile
But of course that idea was not in their mind
They were off like a shot with more booty to find

On the porch was a pumpkin with flashing lights bright
Which broke up the darkness of such a fine night.
And let the proud parents who stood far away
Know their children were safe on this dark scary day

The bright orange field pumpkins that stood on the stairs
Got only slight notice and never long glares
They let the kids know that this house was quite dandy
And willing and ready to give out fine candy

Many neighbours appeared with their children in hand
Resplendent in costume and looking quite grand
Their children were giggly, and happy, and loud
Both sides of the family all felt very proud

I hope that this season that comes once a year
Will still make us all want to stand up and give cheer
To know that the witches and kings by the score
Will last for the day and forever and more

Happiness is the way

There is no better time to be happy
Happiness is the way
Carve a new path that you have set forth
To ensure a happy day

It starts when you open your eyes in the morn
With a smile that brightens your face
You feel right on track as you plan out your day
And hope you can keep up the pace

Good deeds at times don't come easy
With too many things on your mind
When you're searching for ways to be happy
Or you're searching for ways to be kind

Happiness often lies dormant
When it hasn't been used in awhile
But it doesn't take long to emerge once again
And to reproduce a big smile

And that, my good friends, is all that it takes
To bring mirth to someone you meet
In a small café you pass on your way
Or someone you meet on the street

Nod and say hi like you know them
And maybe you did in the past
It doesn't much matter just how you say hi
The image continues to last

Happiness is the way to stay fit
Your strength will emerge from your smile
The more that you give, the more you get back
So you can go the extra mile

Have You Ever Ignored Your Gut And Regretted It?

One day when I was fifty
My wife took me aside
She asked if I would drive her
To the country for a ride

I answered in the positive
And my interest was quite peeked
I was keen to see what she had planned
And when I learned, I freaked

Skydiving was her mission
And her son would be her guide
He would jump with her in tandem
All strapped in for a smooth ride

My gut told me to stay on earth
And don't be such a fool
I had a very strong desire
And it really would be cool

I watched them from the ground below
As they sailed into the air
And when the chutes burst open
It was grand beyond compare

I had my chance to jump with her
And regret my gut reaction
But watching her descend to earth
Gave me great satisfaction

The summer is here and the warmth fills my soul
I feel I just kicked a great winning goal
A goal that will last and strengthen my heart
I am not at the end; I am just at the start

Hearing at last

I used to try to guess the words
When in a conversation
I often got in trouble
And was left in consternation

I didn't want to face the facts
About my loss of sound
It didn't suit my image
And was also quite profound

I went to an Audiologist
To get myself checked out
I wanted to confirm at least
Bad hearing or "The gout"

I was put into a soundproof room
With a window for a view
To identify and quantify
The things I had to do

My hearing loss was terrible
Especially in one ear
I was always saying pardon
If people were not near

That was many years ago
I'm on my third pair now
I received them at Oak Bay Hearing
And I give them a big WOW

The receptionist who greets you
Is a treasure you'll adore
And Dr. Erin Wright, who tests you
Will be friends forever more

Hugging

When I sense you lying beside me
I feel all of your warmth from within
And much like a moth with a brand new cocoon
You feel like a layer of skin

A skin that shields and protects me
A skin that is fueled with desire
Your touch is so hot that it boils my blood
Like a Hindu funeral pyre

The comfort of having you ever so near
Brings joy outside of my realm
My senses are maxed to the limit
With someone else at the helm

Out of control with desire
Out of control with my needs
Leaves me wanton and ravaged completely
That your love continually feeds

How can love support such desires?
Did the arrow from Cupid hit home?
Is it lodged in my chest like an anchor?
Secure and to never more roam?

New love is all of the things that I've said
New love sets our hearts on fire
New love is a vessel of unrepressed joy
And we feel like we're stuck in a mire

Take hold of this feeling whenever you can
It's ephemeral and fleeting for sure
But I know for certain when love hits your heart
That it's wonderful, caring, and pure

I miss your kisses

Oh My Gosh, I miss your kisses
Cause they complete all my three wishes
They fill my day with pure delight
And guide me to the edge of night

I miss you in the opposite chair
A bobby pin stuck in your hair
A smile that keeps my coffee hot
And warms the pewter ginger pot

You read the news and pass it on
And it is still the break of dawn
I have the day to feast my eyes
To catch your look of pure surprise

I love the time we spend alone
Together or upon the phone
Connecting in so many ways
That helps my heart keep off the glaze

My thoughts of you are so enchanted
I never take your heart for granted
With deep respect, I hold you near
To comfort you and call you dear

It still seems like a fairy tale
With joy that fills a giant pail
It's full right to the upper rim
It's always bright and never dim

I know that I'm a minute man
Just loving you the best I can
I hope our hearts are touching, my friend
Respect and love and hugs, amen

I'd Rather Die Full of Pie

I'd rather die full of pie and be happy
And to know that I made the right choice
Feeling fully content with the sweetness
And allowing my thoughts their own voice

How often does one get to speak their own voice?
And state what they mean with conviction
It feels so darn good at the moment
That it's almost a sense of addiction

By doing so more than we ought to
It allows us the freedom of speech
So we don't tag along with the others
And hang on like a freshwater leech

Being one of the crowd is a good thing
And for many, that's all they can do
If they try to exert a true sense of self
They always end up feeling blue

I'm not trying to say that standing alone
Is the ultimate statement of choice?
It's like trying to decide the car you will drive
A Ferrari or brand-new Rolls Royce

Do what feels good at the moment
It can't hurt to be stubborn in view
Decisions are often a choice from the past
And not something that's all about you

Exert your feelings the way that you wish
Feel blessed for the sun and the sky
Remembering why I started this poem
I'd much rather die full of pie

It Is All Within

Why does it matter?
The colour of our skin?
For all that really matters
Is neatly tucked within

Not inside a closet
Where it mingles with the shirts
Or locked up in a soap jar
Where it just comes out in squirts

Not inside a castle wall
With a moat to keep you out
Where a whisper falls on deaf ears
And it makes you want to shout

Not inside an oak tree
That is covered all in bark
Where it soon can turn to ashes
With a tiny little spark

Not inside an apple
That makes you want to squirm
Where your eyes are fully focused
On a partially eaten worm

Not inside a bank vault
Where our money feels at home
Or on the mighty prairies
Where the bison tend to roam

The thoughts that tend to make us whole
And fill our hearts with pride
Are the ones we keep inside us?
As we take this magic ride

Labour Day weekend

What a day to celebrate in early September
With the kids so excited to start
Some for the first time, some for the last
And the energy off of the chart

I remember my children starting school
Excited and afraid both together
Not knowing the rules of the road, so to speak
And yet feeling ever so clever

The journey of life is one we all take
No option about stopping the train
It just keeps on chugging and pushing out smoke
And repeats it again and again

I've taken the challenge so many times
And I've found that each time that I change
It gives me a lift for the better
And I feel like I'm home on the range

One thing that I've learned as age settles in
Is that kindness is just like a drug
So when meeting a person and shaking their hand
I try if I can for a hug

Just try it and see if it works as I say
It will lift you right off of your feet
The hugs will flow in like your Santa
When you're boisterous or when you're discreet

Each day I am thankful for all that I have
My health and my humour abound
I'm not starting school like the children
But I'm glad for the love I have found

Last Rainy Day in November

The rain outside my window
Has stopped as the wind fills its place
Removing the leaves from the branches
Without any pretense of grace

Some of the leaves seemed glued to their spot
Holding on like mother to child
While others depart in an instant
Feeling listless but aiming for wild

Are we not like the leaf in so many ways?
Holding on till our last breath has left
Feeling like we are a burden
Alone and often bereft

Many leaves stay on till the bitter end
Refusing to give up the fight
The last drop of sap is still holding on
And makes the endurance seem right

How like the leaf our life often seems
As we fit in the lot carved in stone
Afraid to branch out and reach for the sky
And end up by our self all alone

I'm here to tell you there are other ways
To travel through life my good friends
Adjust to the joys you have chosen
Instead of with lots of amends

The wind is blowing the rain away
As the sun burns a hole in the sky
The day smells just right as I tie up my shoes
Like a freshly baked granny smith pie

Last Saturday of September

I left my blinds wide open
When I went to sleep last night
So in the early morning
The sun burst through with pure delight

I wandered to the window
Still amazed at the light beams within
They reflected my inner feelings
Like a sparkle bouncing off of a tin

What a wonderful way to start the day
With a light beam that shines from above
Filling my soul with warmth so divine
And flooding my body with love

Many days are great to live in
When your heart does what it should
When it pulses to your rhythm
Like it's made from living wood

When your mind expands to take it in
And fills your life with joy
You revert from being an adult
And become a childish boy

I've found it doesn't take a lot
To let the sunshine in
To let your worries leave you
And forget about your sin

Give thanks today for what you have
Let others know your glee
And you will find before too long
They'll be resting on your knee

Learning Spanish
August 22 2017

It has been a long time
Since I tried to set a task
While in another country
Learning how to talk and ask

I wasn't very good at school
When languages were taught
My brain just wouldn't function
And the words just never caught

I'm trying now to rectify
My errors from the past
But bad habits seem to linger
And the die it seems is cast

I go to school three days a week
With seniors of my age
But the words still don't grab me
And stay stuck upon the page

I try my best to do the tasks
Assigned when class is over
But the words still seem elusive
Like a missing four-leaf clover

Can it be true our learning fades
As the twilight years begin
Cause it often seems to take more time
To end up with a win

I plan to study for the course
And finish with the rest
But it sure has made me think a lot
And put me to the test

Lifeline of Love

You are my lifeline of love
That keeps me together each day
That draws me in close when I'm lonely
And never turns me away

You always carry me forward
Like foam on the incoming tide
And fill up my heart till its bursting
With love and compassion, and pride

There is no need to be lonely
There is no need to be sad
When you touch my hand upon meeting
The main emotion is glad

Glad that we met with friendship in mind
Glad we became such good friends
We trust one another completely
With never a need for amends

AMEN sums you up in one simple word
SO BE IT just trips off my tongue
Reminding me how I feel about you
Because you are the lottery I won

You are the dove for my turtle
You are the shine of my sun
You are the wonder of wonderful
Because you are the sum of just ONE

I give thanks each day when I open my eyes
And I realize that you are so near
To hold me and hug me and call me your own
When you utter the words ROBIN DEAR

Listening

We take our ears for granted
And the sounds that they collect
We add it to our memory
And then try to recollect

In one ear and out the other
Is a catch phrase often used
To describe when words are spoken
But the listener is confused

When I listen to something I don't understand
My mind becomes a blank
I need it all repeated
To fill up my memory tank

And when the tank is full again
And thoughts start leaking out
They rush to exit quickly
Like water from a spout

I try my best to catch the words
That always fill the air
And when I yell out "pardon"
I get a haughty stare

My hearing aids are going wild
No dials left to turn
And as the noise builds up inside
My ears begin to burn

I listen like I think I should
Both ears are open wide
I try to take it in all I hear
And thump my chest with pride

WARING JONES

Little Ditty

A mouse got caught in a corner
He was scared as scared could be
He held his breath and closed his eyes
And counted from one to three

He kept them both closed for a very long time
In hopes that his luck would change
Hoping the cat would disappear
And that he would be out of range

As luck would have it that Friday morn
His luck turned out to be real
He opened his eyes to discover
And saw what he could not feel

The cat was eating from its' cat food bowl
And had no interest in mice
The mouse was grateful beyond belief
And finished up eating his rice

The mouse was relieved to be living
After having such a big scare
He was feeling so lucky beyond belief
And glad that he wasn't served rare

The problem remained about staying alive
As he made his way back to his home
It was under the stove in the kitchen
From where he would never more roam

He took a dep breath and made a mad dash
Zig zagging until he was home
He closed up the hole with a dried out old prune
And for safety he added some foam

Long Walk in San Miguel
September 13 2017

The streets in San Miguel Allende
Are really very bumpy
If the city were a mattress
You would call it very lumpy

I set out on this sunny day
To find a certain street
And what a bumpy walk I had
That turned out oh so neat

I had my sandals done up tight
All ready for the stroll
It didn't take me very long
Till I was on a roll

The miles kept on piling on
The street I sought was found
I didn't feel like heading back
And turn myself around

I had some food at a little place
And we talked about his life
About being Mexican in the U. S. A.
That was filled with so much strife

I explored so many streets today
And met four friends I knew
I saw a different side of life
I'm not accustomed too

I kept on walking in the sun
To see what I might find
And in the end when all was done
I found some piece of mind

Longer days

As winter grips us with the cold
And frost puts on a sheen
I try to be quite positive
And not be in between

The days are getting longer
So I know that spring is near
Its many months away of course
But I shift another gear

A gear that helps change my desire
Of curling up at home
And waiting for a message
To pop up on my new phone

I rather like the thought
Of cruising round the town
And chatting up all those I meet
While acting as a clown

A clown brings out the best in me
And lets my thoughts be freely spoken
And not be bundled up inside
Like an unused subway token

I try to be as giving
In the messages that I pass on
So that my thoughts I speak so freely
Will be like fish eggs as they spawn

Be kind to everyone you meet
We know not what a person has to say
But whatever message emerges
It will surely make our day

Love

Love is like a bright red scarf
That wraps around your head
It keeps you warm and cozy
So you don't feel any dread

It keeps the love from leaking out
And spoiling your day
Like a horse stuck in its narrow stall
Without a bale of hay

Or a runner at the starting gate
That can't find any blocks
To spur them to the finish line
And knock off someone's socks

Love also helps the day go by
With kindness and reflection
And steers us like a pilot would
To keep the right direction

A direction that is helpful
To those who need it most
Keeps the love you've given freely
To remain a perfect host

We all need lots of guidance
And love to keep us strong
To stay the straight and narrow
As we try to do no wrong

A love that has no boundaries
Is the scarf we all should wear
Giving hugs to all we cherish
And to show how much we care

March 1st

A brand new month a brand new day
A grey and cloudy sky
If I were having guests tonight
I'd make an apple pie

An apple pie can set the mood
For what the day might bring
Especially at this time of year
When it is almost spring

Spring is in the air at last
The winter was so cold
It's been the worst in many years
At least that's what I'm told

The flowers are trying to do their best
By breaking through the ground
To spread their wondrous colours
And let more of them abound

It's three weeks before the solstice
And the days begin to lengthen
The buds burst out profusely
And their branches start to strengthen

The trees have dropped their last lone leaves
No need to hold on now
Since bright green buds are forming
That makes us shout out "wow"

Spring Is just around the corner
I can smell it in the air
And as the poet Ovid said
"Enter ye who dare"

Meeting for the first time

The dishes are done and all put away
I have just finished the most marvelous day
It started at seven with early sunshine
Then lunch that included some very dry wine

My family and friends arrived right on time
To share in the feast that was varied and fine
To top it all off I had fresh apple pie
With whip cream on top piled up to the sky

I had made a commitment a few days before
To hook up with a lady and meet about four
To see if our meeting would garner attention
To carry us forward and have some retention

I am always unsure on the first little date
Comparing each other to see how we rate
Unsure what will happen as time marches on
From morning till evening and night until dawn

Two spirits unsure of what to do next
Talking receiving and sending out text
To help clarify the thoughts in one's head
And hoping you feel content and not dread

We both ordered coffee to help break the ice
She seemed quite delightful in fact very nice
Our shyness was gone our smiles filled the space
We soon both agreed we should enter the race

Time has a way to bring couples together
When heavy regrets turn into a feather
When guidance prevails to show us the way
And gives us a reason to leave or to stay

Melting Snow in Victoria British Columbia
February 10 2017

The snow is melting in a rush
All that's left is cold wet slush
Reminding us of what has been
And the beauty we have seen

It took the City by surprise
Transforming it before our eyes
The streets were turned from grey to white
By blanketing the grimy blight

It gave us all some thoughts to ponder
So once again we walk and wander
Returning to our daily lives
Like bees inside their honeyed hives

The leaden branches that once were sagging
Start to spring back as if they're bragging
Resplendent with their buds so green
With drops of snow left in between

I venture forth on slippery ruts
Hoping to see some fishing huts
While snowmen dot the countryside
With head and body full of pride

Kids and adults roll mounds of snow
Yelling and happy as they go
Thinking their new found friends will last
As if a concrete die were cast

But in the morn when they arise
The snow has melted before their eyes
And in its place a dark green bud
That thrills us so and churns our blood

Morning thoughts

I often awake from a great evenings sleep
Lying in bed with my thoughts
I don't feel like breakfast, or coffee, and such
And I sure don't want to do squats

I am just about to turn eighty
I can hardly believe it myself
Many a person at my age
Is already put on the shelf

I guess that my genes are doing their job
By keeping me healthy and fit
There is no pain when I stand or bend over
And no pain when I walk or I sit

My left shoulder is giving me trouble
So I favour the right one instead
And I lie on my back when I'm sleeping
In my cozy and warm double bed

What gifts I've been given to help me survive
All the hardships we face day to day
The food costs the rent the friends that are gone
I'm lucky-- what more can I say

When I look around and see what I have
I feel thankful for being alive
Able to still do some pushups
And to jump in my car and then drive

Thank you thank you thank you
Are words I repeat all the time
They help me to keep myself grounded
And to know that I'm doing just fine

Music

When music plays the earth stands still
It shifts upon its' axis
It's like your accountant informing you
This year you owe no taxes

How can that be you wonder?
As you act with great surprise
Of course it thrills you greatly
As the tears fill up your eyes

Is that a nocturne I just heard?
To me it doesn't matter
It's not like idle gossip
Full of nonsense and dull chatter

The conductor enters center stage
Anxiety picks up its' tempo
Will it be a fast allegro?
Or a softer decrescendo

It matters not to those involved
Each note is known by heart
It envelopes everyone concerned
From the ending to the start

The music thrills the audience
Who've heard it all before
Many know the tiny details
Of the complicated score

When music took its' hold on me
When I was just a lad
I thank the stars it happened
For I always feel so glad

My lover my partner my friend

I think of you often my sweet darling Liz
And the love that the two of us share
The spark that ignites whenever we touch
Demonstrates just how much we both care

We spark like a balloon with friction
We spark like a wand for the BBQ
We spark like the stars on a dark dark sky
And I spark with my love for you

Being a partner in all that we do
Reminds me that we are together
We cook and we play and we have great fun
And it feels very much like a tether

A partner has many function I feel
To care for each other's needs
Console when occasions demand it
And dress wounds when your partner bleeds

Thank you so much for holding my hand
At the doctor's office last week
A selfless act from a warm loving sole
Without making me feel meek

A friend has many functions to fill
And you Liz have filled me right up
There is no room left to measure
In your wonderful loving cup

Being your lover always makes me alive
So the two of us act as if one
I melt in your arms every time we embrace
And it always turns out to be fun

WARING JONES

New friends

I always enjoy meeting new friends
One never knows what you'll find
It could be a relative or a long lost friend
Or a friend of a similar mind

There are so many friends who want to be found
To enjoy the company you give
Some you will like and some you will not
And some who say live and let live

Life is too short to be squandered
By casting aspersions galore
There is no need to be hurtful
Or to try and even the score

A new friend always brings a new challenge
A challenge you face with aplomb
And when the dust settles and things become clear
We all go out for dim sum

I have to admit that that I crave for attention
To keep up my spirits in gear
And not to hold back about goals unattained
Or to cringe at goals that I fear

New input from friends tends to stoke all my fires
So hot that my skin turns to red
And when I cool down from excitement
No path is blocked where I tread

Thank you for being a new friend to me
A friend who will widen my view
A friend who will broaden my outlook
A friend I would like to pursue

Ocean Waves

I must go down to the seas again
Is a very apt expression
It draws us there like a magnet
Reaching out in our direction

I love to watch the ocean
With its' waves so much like thunder
Beckoning us to its' rocky shores
And begging to draw us under

I couldn't hear the sounds it made
While crashing on the shore
I was tucked inside my auto
With a locked and soundproof door

I enjoy the oceans power
And the constant changing tide
And the thrilled and chilled wind surfers
As they take their well earned ride

They power up to the edge of the wave
And stop to get their thrill
And proceed to ride the roiling surf
And hope for the best that they will

The wind subsides---a calm appears
No reason for the lull
It's all just part of the changing scene
Of a view that's never dull

The Ocean waves came crashing down
Upon the pebbled beach
They were all wrapped up in silence
And were too far out of reach

I was a sailor on the Great Lake Tankers for two summers when I was a teenager. I never tired of being on the ocean or the Great Lakes and the power that water holds. One evening on Georgian Bay the wheelhouse was breached by a wave that broke through the glass and steel and almost sank our ship. I knew then why Gordon Lightfoot wrote the song The Edmund Fitzgerald

Old friends

Old friends are always with you
In their spirit and desire
They can't just be extinguished
Like the coals of a red hot fire

Old friends helped to form our building blocks
Giving strength when we needed it most
Allowing us to plow ahead
So we wouldn't dawdle and coast

Old friends will never leave you
When you fail in what you're after
They help to keep the storms away
Like a sturdy roofing rafter

Old friends will take your elbow
And then guide you to your table
With no rewards expected
Such as platinum or sable

Old friends are what you think of first
When recalling bygone days
No fog surrounds your memories
That leave you in a haze

Old friends need no reminders
Of your treasures from the past
They are chiseled out like granite
That you know will always last

Old friends remain old friends
From the crib up to the coffin
To call upon when needed
Be it once or be it often

Perfect

Perfect perfect perfect
Is the way our love has been
From the first time that we ever met
With no differences in between

There was no warm up needed
No pleasantries to start
We touched we kissed we made great love
No horse before the cart

The magic of the moment
Has become a love divine
We encourage truth and honesty
And it's all worked out just fine

Each morn when I awake
Lying cozy in my bed
My first thought turns to you my love
About what we've thought and said

I'm thankful for the love we have
And how we blend as one
With all of our endeavors
Ending up as so much fun

Meeting friends is so rewarding
When our new friends meet to dine
And results in such a perfect mix
Like a blended good French wine

Perfect perfect perfect
Is the way our love has grown
I am so thankful for your presence
And the love that you have shown

Please share your heart with me

Please share your heart with me
And I'll share my heart with you
And with this constant sharing
We will find a love anew

A love like none before us
A love that's sure to last
Giving strength to push us forward
Without drawing on the past

This new love will unite us
As we form new ties that bind
Always joining us together
In our spirit and our mind

There are always peaks and valleys
In our search for new found goals
And we will navigate together
To avoid the hidden shoals

Mistakes are sure to happen
In this journey of the heart
And each one will be conquered
To provide a brand new start

A new found quest will rear its' head
And walls will surely crumble
Deflating loving egos
And a sense of feeling humble

Please share you heart with me
And I'll guard it with my soul
I will share my heart with you
And two halves will form a whole

Rain at night

The rain keeps pounding the darkened night
Like a surf that cannot find its shore
Relentlessly searching to end its big roll
But keeps pounding and pounding once more

It seems that the wind has a mind of its own
When driving the droplets to earth
It gets all caught up like a personal joke
With deceit and wonder and mirth

The rain lets up for a minute or two
Not sure of what to do next
It's not like it has a script to live by
Or to follow along with some text

The noise starts to soften and calm itself down
Like a train when it pulls to a stop
And then it starts up like a ravaging bull
Or volcano that's ready to pop

I'm always in wonder when nature takes hold
And continues the journey it's planned
We still have no say to predict the next move
Our best efforts seem hopelessly banned

I don't mind the rain, or the wind that ensues
Cuz It helps me sometimes when I'm resting
I feel cozy and safe in my own little world
Like a duck on its egg when it's nesting

The wind has all gone to where I don't know
I miss it when I go to sleep
So I'll just turn my head a little this way
And I promise I won't make a peep

Rose Petal Dropping

A rose petal fell to my table
From a vase that it perfectly fit
It lies resolute in its splendor
Determined to blend in and submit

The vase was designed many years ago now
By my wife when she was quite young
She designed and built many fine pieces
Some were practical and some were for fun

It had not been fired when she was alive
She had others that fit the same bill
They were wrapped up in storage for many long years
And to see them complete was a thrill

Kit died in February of twenty nine-teen
Her dementia had taken its toll
It was able to capture her body
But unable to capture her sole

I had no idea of the treasures she made
As each object emerged from the kiln
Presenting a picture of years that had passed
Much like clips from a black and white film

To me they are precious and filled with her love
Like the clay that she molded so well
Depicting her thoughts of days that have gone
And making my heart start to swell

Each object she made brings joy to my heart
Provoking a feeling that lingers
And I realize as I take them in hand
They were made by her supple fingers

WARING JONES

That's What You'd Do

When I was a child you propped me up
You gave me food and you filled my cup
You showed me games I never knew
When I was child that's what you'd do

And now that you are gone
I'm left alone to carry on
And I can't forget how you made me see
I was part of you and you were part of me

When I was teen you gave me strength
You went to all almost any length
You showed me how to start anew
When I was teen that's what you do

And now that you are gone
I'm left alone to carry on
And I can't forget how you made me see
I was part of you and you were part of me

Now I'm a man and the memories remain
There's still an ache and a yearning pain
A longing want to be with you
Now I'm a man that's what you do

And now that you are gone
I'm left alone to carry on
And I can't forget how you made me see
I was part of you and you were part of me

The Human Touch

Feeling the warmth of the human touch
Always feels so loving to me
Like a baby clutching your finger
Or being gently bounced on your knee

Human touch reminds me
Of my mother holding my hand
As I took my very first walking steps
And feeling ever so grand

Hugs of course are high on the list
Of wonderful feelings within
It is hard not to feel the loving
As a frown turns into a grin

A handshake brings a sense of belonging
That minutes before wasn't there
Much like the feeling when sitting
When someone has pulled out you chair

The human touch need not be grand
Like a trumpet that welcomes a king
A simple nod of acknowledgment
Can sometimes do the same thing

When one reaches out for your elbow
To help guide you through a small crowd
Is often a sign of true caring
Without being boastful or loud

Try touching your loved ones as much as you can
The rewards are repaid in pure gold
A constant reminder of love that has been
And brings memories when you are old

The Messiah

And his name shall be called
Wonderful Counselor, Mighty God
Everlasting Father, Prince of Peace

What a way to start the season
By listening to a choir
The more they sing the better it gets
And it keeps on going higher

Christmas for me as a Christmas child
Was having Handel played every day
Our family would sing at the top of our lungs
And trying our best not to spray

The Messiah has become such a standard
Some children know the words as rote
They can handle the singing quite nicely
Just like an often used quote

It was a very cold evening last week
As the crowd gathered for the occasion
The theater was filled to the rafters
And was more like a soccer invasion

When the symphony struck the first chords
The music filled us with joy
The rustling of clothing had stopped
And once again I became a young boy

As the wonderful music filled the air
Many memories began to flood in
Recalling the words in an instant
And mouthing them much like a hymn

Rejoice rejoice rejoice greatly
O daughter of Zion
And let Handle be played
And go out like a lion

The sound of your voice

The sound of hearing your voice
Is a sound that's too hard to measure
It thrills me each time that you talk
And it's like finding long buried treasure

I've never found buried treasure
My pirate days are all over
But I surmise from what I've heard
It's like rolling in the clover

Your voice denotes the coming of spring
Like flowers about to burst open
There are no words to describe it
Or my feelings after you've spoken

Your soft Irish trill fills me with glee
When whispered each time that we touch
No matter how often it happens
I still get a warm fuzzy flush

When two people feel the way that we do
After searching but not satisfied
It feels so delightful in every respect
That we then take it all in our stride

I don't take it lightly the love that we have
Your comfort is more than just touch
We have both accepted each other
With no feeling to hurry or rush

My lover, my partner, my friend
Encapsulates the way that I feel
No words really have the power
To show that our love is for real

Thinking of you this morning

I was thinking of you this morning
Eating my berries and cream
I felt so delighted I started to smile
Knowing we're such a great team

We both have a strong sense of honour
To ourselves and the one by our side
Who helps us in what we desire
And to show we're not here for the ride

To love one another takes more than just trust
It takes spirit and similar goals
To fight incoming waves with a passion
And avoid the sharp silent shoals

The unexpected is just round the bend
As relationships grow and expand
But life throws us curves like a baseball
And things don't always go as we planned

When I think of you and you're not around
It's the small stuff that stokes up my fire
A soft warm embrace as I enter your home
Always warms my heart with desire

I never get tired of you by my side
As we sit on the couch for a game
It doesn't much matter the game that we play
I'm the candle and you are the flame

My flame keeps getting stronger
Each time that we meet and we touch
We are like a car that's in motion
Some gas some brake and some clutch

Thinking of you

One of the many wonderful joys about love
Is the joy of remembering you
Not just your features and bountiful hugs
But the wonderful things that you do

Each time I arrive at your door for a date
A welcoming kiss greets my lips
A touch on the shoulder confirms you are near
And I feel like we're joined at the hips

We two become one in an instant
A unit of love and desire
Neither one of acts as a chorus
We transform to a beautiful choir

The music we make is part of our love
A love that both of us treasure
It lifts our spirits to a higher plateau
And fills us both with pleasure

Respect and understanding
Connects us both together
It is paramount in our beliefs
And acts just like a tether

Our love is mightier than the sword
Or a cage that keeps you captured
As we grow closer every day
We feel even more enraptured

That is why I think of you
Each eve and early dawn
You give me strength and love divine
To help me carry on

Thoughts

Some of the thoughts that we bring to the table
Should never be spoken out loud
Critical thoughts are not welcome
And should not be thought of as proud

Be true to your word as much as you can
And give praise at the drop of a hat
It does wonders for everyone's ego
And is really where it's all at

Shine brightly as much as you can
And show others the path you have found
They can then carry on in your absence
Just in case that you're not around

The more that you smile at others
The more they'll smile back at you
Every smile helps to fill your loving cup
That is fresh as cool morning dew

Try to remember each time that you speak
That most people enjoy what you say
Be thoughtful and kind with your wording
And not simply to "have a good day"

A light touch on somebodies shoulder
Lets them understand that you care
It may seem quite simple after the fact
But to them is really quite rare

Hug when you can when occasion permits
Let the energy run through your veins
It feels like a cleansing has just set you free
And you've just taken hold of the reins

Together

You and I belong to each other
We knew it right from the start
It seems cupid had his arrows lined up
And shot us both through the heart

Our hearts responded in kind
And joined us together as one
Knowing full well the gift that we have
As each thread is carefully spun

Each thread that is spun makes us stronger
No matter how thin or how frail
Each one reinforcing the other
So that love will win out and prevail

A task such as this does not falter
Or leave sadness and trouble behind
It gathers momentum forever
Without feeling caught or confined

We grow by the day and the hour
Revealing our thoughts and our prayers
One foot in front of the other
While climbing a life full of stairs

Each step reveals new emotions
Some hidden and others on view
Some thoughts are forward and simple
While others are often askew

Think not of the lessons that we have both learned
Or the magic our love brings to us
Just know that I love you forever
No troubles, no fighting, no fuss

Two Fairies

I have two fairies guarding my house
They dangle at the front door
They've been stationed there for a year or two
And I hope for a few years more

I love the way that they twist with the wind
When the door opens up for a guest
I like them at night time with light on their backs
It's probably the time I like best

I never get tired of watching them twirl
They seem both allusive and near
I never get tired of watching them swing
As they always bring me good cheer

It seems rather strange the comfort they give
Two slim silhouettes on a thread
But they stave off the demons from coming inside
And bring joy and good fortune instead

They remind me of how our own active lives
Often dangle above the abyss
As we all try our best to figure things out
So that nothing's left out or gets missed

It's getting quite dark outside my front door
I better go check that they're fine
I don't want to find that they've fallen apart
And are dangling there on the line

Are we like the fairies each day that we live
A shadow of what we once were
Or are we bold and brave and sure of ourselves
So that nothing real bad can occur

WARING JONES

Welcoming the day

It's dark outside my window
And the birds seem very calm
They're waiting for the sun to rise
To welcome in the dawn

The grass is laden with the dew
The green and brown together
It's trying hard to stay alive
In all this hot and sunny weather

Another perfect day it seems
Is trying to break out
And likely will succeed I'm sure
In spite of all this drought

Hot weather on the island
Brings joy beyond compare
And lifts our mood immensely
So we want to give and share

I'm more than thankful everyday
When blue skies gently merge
It makes me want to jump with joy
And adds an extra surge

Thank heavens that I have my health
And friends that bring me joy
And help me to remember
My memories as a boy

Old memories fade in all of us
And new ones come a knocking
It's how we keep our spirits up
And keep our lives a rocking

What a nice day to die
February 4 2019

What a nice day to die
With the snow falling down to the ground
What a nice day to die
With my family all gathered around

What a nice day to die
And to end all this suffering at last
What a nice day to die
I am sorry it didn't go fast

I've been locked up inside this body of mine
Unable to talk or decide
I have listened with love and great patience
But was only along for the ride

The care I have had is unrivaled
From day one to my last gasp of air
Please thank all the help at the lodging
Everyone always took such great care

Jamie and Robin took most of the pain
With Tonya and others as well
My heart felt broken so often
And with no way to break the sad spell

It is finally over dear family
I have left all my loved ones behind
No more guessing of when it will happen
And I thank you for being so kind

What a nice day to die lovely people
I will love you till we meet again
And when that day comes in the future
I'll be there to welcome you in

When love sits on your shoulder

When love sits on your shoulder
The world is a magical place
There are no frowns or wrinkles
On anybody's face

The sky is always azure blue
The sun a mighty boulder
The clouds just seem to disappear
When love sits on your shoulder

The birds tweet softly in your ear
Each morning as you rise
And fill your heart near bursting
And it comes as no surprise

Long sorrows fade into the dark
And ice cream seems much colder
The twinkle of your eyes increase
When love sits on your shoulder

Each time you touch your special love
Mere words they just can't capture
The joy of what you're feeling
Is not just joy but total rapture

When love sits on your shoulder
And the moon hangs in the sky
There is no thought of questions
Or to ask the reason why

The moment stays forever
As your arms reach out to hold her
And your life is full of wonder
When love sits on your shoulder

Yellow Butterfly

I see you at times in your butterfly disguise
As you flit from flower to flower
I remember the times when I needed you most
And you held me for hour after hour after hour

It didn't much matter the hurt that I had
You held me until I was better
You snuggled me close to your bosom
In a blouse but sometimes a sweater

Those tender moments of kindness
Still linger and offer me strength
Reminding me of a mothers love
And how you went to any length

I know that at times you were torn
Between saving the hurt that I felt
Or to let me peruse the path I was on
And deal with the cards I was dealt

Saving a child from hardship
Is never a task easily taken
You want to step in and lighten the load
So your child does not feel forsaken

The path that we take on our journey
Is one that is fraught with much sorrow
We see only today and what it may bring
With no thoughts for the night or tomorrow

I miss you dear Pearl and the love that you gave
It sustains me each day that I rise
You showed me the paths to be taken
And bring tears to my brown loving eyes

Yellow Rosebud

A beautiful yellow rosebud
Fell from the bush in the garden bed
It landed quite close to my foot print
It was yellow and all trimmed in red

The petals were curled oh so tightly
Each layer all ready to bloom
I picked up the bud and brought it inside
Inside to a brightly lit room

The stem was quite short but seemed strong for its size
So I placed it inside a small vase
There was no reaction for more than a day
But to me there was more than just cause

I filled up the vase with warm water
Cut the stem so it fit nice and tight
And set it beside a black placemat
So the setting would look oh so right

This morning it started its journey
As the petals began to unfurl
I am watching it open in wonder
And hope that the petals don't curl

Its' beauty is locked in the moment
For me to enjoy at my will
I am glad that I kept the small rosebud
It has given me such a great thrill

As each layer reveals the beauty within
It shows off the treasures we hide
Come take my hand and allow me
To be your self-loving guide

Morning Sun

The sun shone through my window
Like shards of broken gold
To welcome in the morning
And a day that's bright and cold

So cold it makes me shiver
As my feet touch on the floor
But the warmth of wooly slippers
Helps to even up the score

As I saunter down the stairway
The heat is flowing up
And keeps me in good spirits
Till I have my first hot cup

And when the cup touches my lips
With liquid dark and hot
It reminds me of the adage
"It really hits the spot"

The sun to show its power
Makes the kitchen warm and bright
It sparkles like a diamond
And eliminates the night

I love this time of the day best
When all is calm and bright
It helps to keep me centered
And that things will be all right

A time when thoughts are open
And a new day has begun
Feeling blessed and oh so grateful
For my friends and for the sun

CPSIA information can be obtained
at www.ICGtesting.com
Printed in the USA
LVHW031334100323
741314LV00001B/1